FAMOUS U.S. AIR FORCE BOMBERS

FAMOUS U.S. AIR FORCE BOMBERS

David C. Cooke

Dodd, Mead & Company   New York

PICTURE CREDITS

Boeing Aircraft, p. 18, 24 (bottom), 25 (bottom), 38, 39, 52 (center), 58, 59 (center), 64 (top left)

Peter M. Bowers, p. 24 (top), 34 (top)

Convair, p. 30, 31, 48, 49, 50, 51 (top, bottom), 60, 61

Curtiss-Wright, p. 10, 12, 13, 16 (top), 17 (right), 40, 41, 64 (bottom left)

Douglas Aircraft, p. 26, 27 (bottom), 28, 34 (bottom), 42, 43 (top left, right), 62

Harold Kulick, p. 27 (top), 63

Howard Levy, p. 17 (left)

Lockheed Aircraft, p. 45

McDonnell Aircraft, p. 59 (top)

The Martin Co., p. 8, 9, 20 (left), 36

North American Aviation, p. 32, 33 (top), 54

Northrop Aircraft, p. 23

Pratt & Whitney Aircraft, p. 52 (top)

Ryan Aeronautical, p. 43 (bottom)

Smithsonian Institution, p. 16 (bottom)

U.S. Air Force, p. 11, 14, 15, 19, 20 (right), 21, 22, 24 (center), 25 (top, center), 29, 33 (bottom), 35, 37 (top, center), 44, 47, 51 (center), 52 (bottom), 53, 55 (left), 56, 57, 59 (bottom)

Vultee Aircraft, p. 46, 64 (bottom right)

ISBN: 0-396-06695-X
Library of Congress Catalog Card Number: 72-5947
Printed in the United States of America

FOREWORD

The most potent of all warplanes is the bomber, which is designed to carry destruction to the homeland of an enemy, to weaken his ability to wage war. The fighter is mostly defensive; the bomber is meant only for offensive operations. It is the unglamorous workhorse.

The U.S. Air Force today has the most powerful force of bombers in the history of aviation. But this was not always the case. In fact, military aviation was far slower in developing in the United States than in any major country. Until the time of World War I there was not one bomber in this country worthy of the name. When American pilots went into combat in that war, they were forced to fly foreign-designed and foreign-made bombers as well as fighters. Not one American-designed warplane even reached France.

Military aviation in the United States did not begin to develop until after World War I, and for many years progress was slow and designs for new machines were based on outmoded concepts.

Then, almost suddenly it seemed, military aviation in this country shot forward amazingly. The old concepts were tossed aside and originality in design became the keynote.

During its existence the U.S. Air Force has had several changes of name. It came into being on August 1, 1907, as the Aeronautical Division of the Army Signal Corps. In 1914 the Aeronautical Division became the Aviation Section, in 1918 it was renamed Air Service, and eight years later it became the Army Air Corps. In 1941 the name was changed once again to Army Air Forces, and in 1948 independence was finally realized and our land-based air arm became the U.S. Air Force.

This book was designed to present a progressive chronological history of the development of the bomber in the Air Force. There are many gaps, but these were intentional, since I have presented only aircraft which were placed in production. Numerous experimental types were built, but these have been omitted. I have also attempted to include photographs of the various improved models of the airplanes presented.

All of the aircraft on the following pages were entirely of American design. This means that such famous bombers as the De Havilland DH-4 and Martin B-57 Canberra are not included, since both owed their origin to foreign engineers and ingenuity.

Some of the airplanes described were among the most famous bombers ever built, and some were not truly successful. However, each of them contributed at least something to the development of military aviation in the United States.

I have attempted to present an accurate, though brief, story of each of the famous bombers. I trust that the information presented will be useful as well as interesting.

DAVID C. COOKE

5

In memory of three good friends—
Harold Kulick, William "Blimp" Friedman, and Keith Garrison

CONTENTS

The Donald Douglas-designed MB-1 was the first American bomber. It was an outstanding plane for its day.

MARTIN MB-1

During World War I American squadrons in France were equipped entirely with foreign-built or foreign-designed aircraft. Not one American-designed airplane was used in combat.

In an effort to correct this situation, the infant Glenn L. Martin Company was asked to design a bomber that would outperform the British Handley-Page 0/400. Donald Douglas, then a young designer, was given the task of planning the machine.

The officials on the Aircraft Production Board in Washington, D.C., were impressed with the plans of the plane, and they ordered ten models. The first of these was taken up for its first flight tests on August 17, 1918.

The MB-1 was outstanding in most respects. It was not as large as the Handley-Page and carried a smaller bomb load, but it had a higher service ceiling and a faster speed. One of the first ten models was a long-range version with a duration of 1,500 miles, and another mounted a 37-millimeter cannon. Normal armament was five .30-caliber machine guns.

The bomber was too late to see service in World War I, and production was curtailed. Martin built a total of only 14, completing production in 1919.

In 1920 the Army ordered 20 MB-2's, which were similar to the earlier models though with folding wings. Fifteen of these were later redesignated as NBS-1's—Night Bombers, Short Range. These were somewhat larger and slower than the MB-1's, but both the range and bomb load were increased.

While the MB-2's and NBS-1's were never used in warfare, they made blazing headlines. In 1921 Brigadier General William "Billy" Mitchell was challenged by the U.S. Navy to prove his contention that airplanes could sink battleships. On July 18 three of the Martin bombers flew to the test area off the coast of Virginia and sent the former German cruiser *Frankfurt* to the bottom with direct bomb hits.

The 27,000-ton German battleship *Ostfriesland* was the next target. The Navy had claimed that the ship was unsinkable, but on July 21 seven Martin bombers pounded it with 2,000-pound bombs and sank it in less than 22 minutes.

Other data (MB-2): Wing span, 74 feet 2 inches; length, 42 feet 8 inches; loaded weight, 12,075 pounds; engines, two 420-horsepower Liberties; maximum speed, 100 miles per hour at sea level.

An MB-1 over Washington, D.C. Only 34 MB-1's and MB-2's were built, but they were the best Air Service bombers.

CURTISS A-3 FALCON

Following World War I, Congress practically cut off all development funds from the Army, and the Air Service was forced to struggle along with outmoded aircraft, patching them together by whatever means to keep them in flying condition.

This situation could not continue, and in 1924 the Air Service finally received an appropriation of $12,798,576 to purchase new airplanes. One type that was badly needed was a new observation plane, and competitions were held late in 1924 and early the following year.

A Douglas design won the 1924 trials, while Curtiss was one of the losers. Curtiss then made various alterations in its plane, added a new engine, and entered it in the 1925 trials—this time winning.

Curtiss built a number of variations of its original XO-1 Falcon, all in fairly small numbers. Then, in 1927, the Army decided that it required a dif-

The original Curtiss Falcons were classed as observation planes. Four O-1C's were used as personal transports.

A-3A's were similar to the O-1 series, though with two additional guns in the wings. Bomb load was 200 pounds.

ferent type of plane—an attack-bomber. One Douglas O-2 was converted for such duties, but it was not successful. The O-1 Falcon was next altered by the addition of a .30-caliber machine gun in each lower wing panel. With this change, the Falcon became the first American attack-bomber and was designated A-3.

Seventy-five A-3's were built, followed by five A-3A's and 78 A-3B's, all of which were similar.

At best, the machine was not good. It had four forward-firing guns, with two swivel guns in the rear cockpit, and carried 200 pounds of bombs on wing racks. However, the weight of the extra armament lowered its performance well below that of the O-1. But despite these difficulties, the A-3 must go down in the records as the first attack-bomber produced in the United States, thus starting a new trend in military aviation.

Other data (A-3B): Wing span, 38 feet; length, 27 feet 2 inches; loaded weight, 4,458 pounds; engine, 435-horsepower Curtiss D-12; maximum speed, 139 miles per hour at sea level.

The B-2 Condor was the first true long-range strategic bomber for the Air Service. It carried a crew of five.

CURTISS B-2 CONDOR

In 1921, after the designation of the Martin biplane bomber was changed from MB-2 to NBS-1, the Army Air Service asked various manufacturers to submit competitive bids for 100 of the craft. The Curtiss Company underbid Martin, and was given a contract for 50 planes.

With this experience in bombers, Curtiss next produced the XNBS-4 in 1924. The plane was not actually a new concept but an outgrowth of the NBS-1, though considerably larger and with slightly better performance. However, it was not sufficiently improved and was not ordered into production.

Undaunted, Curtiss started to plan its much larger XB-2, which was to develop into the first American strategic bomber. The design concept was similar to the earlier NBS-1 and XNBS-4,

though with important differences. Instead of all-wood construction, Curtiss used duraluminum tubing for both fuselage and wing ribs, with steel spars in the biplane wings and steel tubing in the bomb bay for extra strength. Covering of both fuselage and wings, in the custom of the day, was fabric.

Curtiss also came up with another unusual innovation: an exposed turret in the nacelle behind each engine, with twin .30-caliber guns on swivels. These, plus twin guns in the nose, gave the B-2 the best defensive firepower of any existing bomber. The crew consisted of five men.

The first XB-2 was completed in the late summer of 1927, and the following January a military competition was held at Wright Field. Four airplanes took part in the tests, and the XB-2 came away with all the honors.

The Condor caused something of a battle among

members of the Air Corps Planning Board. Some of the officers wanted to concentrate on the plane for production, while others insisted that only a limited number should be ordered and the extra funds used to purchase the less promising but far more reasonable Keystone LB-6. As it finally worked out, only 12 B-2's were ordered.

The first B-2 was delivered to Wright Field in June, 1929, and the last plane was completed the following January. No others were ordered. The last B-2 was withdrawn from service in May, 1936, at which time it seemed a relic from the past.

Other data: Wing span, 90 feet; length, 47 feet 6 inches; loaded weight, 16,516 pounds; engines, two 600-horsepower Curtiss Conquerors; maximum speed, 132 miles per hour at sea level.

Because of their high cost, only 12 B-2's were ordered. The last of these remained in service until May, 1936.

Keystone's big XB-1A lost out in competition with the Curtiss XB-2. Its performance did not match the Condor's.

KEYSTONE B-3

Huff-Daland was one of the firms which also built the Martin MB-2 (see page 8). With this experience in bombers, the company developed its single-engined XLB-1 (Experimental Light Bomber) in 1923. The Air Service ordered nine production models with 800-horsepower Packard engines and then decided it would prefer a twin-engined version. By the time the XLB-3A was delivered in 1927, the company had been reorganized as the Keystone Aircraft Corporation.

The XLB-3A had two Pratt & Whitney Wasp radial engines of 410 horsepower each. This model was not ordered into production. The first production version was the LB-5, with 420-horsepower Liberty engines, ten of which were built. Another

25 LB-5A's were delivered. These were similar to the LB-5's, except that a twin tail was added in place of the previous single large rudder and two small side rudders.

The plane was produced in a variety of models, all of which were basically similar except for engine changes. Seventeen LB-6's had 525-horsepower Wright Cyclones, and 18 LB-7's mounted 525-horsepower Pratt & Whitney Hornets.

In 1926 the Air Service became the Air Corps, and in 1930 the LB category was discontinued. The 63 LB-10A's then on order were delivered as B-3A's, followed by 25 B-4A's and 39 B-6A's.

During its production life the Keystone bomber's performance was constantly improved. All versions had a crew of five—pilot, co-pilot, bombardier, and two gunners. Armament on some models was three

Keystone received a number of contracts for their LB series. The LB-10A, with 525-h.p. engines, became the B-3A.

.30-caliber guns while others had five guns. The bomb load ranged between 2,000 and 2,500 pounds. The fuselage as well as wings were fabric covered.

Other data (B-6A): Wing span, 74 feet 9 inches; length, 48 feet 10 inches; loaded weight, 13,374 pounds; engines, two 575-horsepower Pratt & Whitney Hornets; maximum speed, 121 miles per hour at sea level.

This is the B-5A. All the Keystone bombers were similar, and they were slow. The B-5A could do only 110 m.p.h.

Two views of the A-8, the first all-metal, low-wing monoplane in the Air Corps. The plane was designed for low-level operations in support of ground troops.

CURTISS A-12 SHRIKE

Following World War I military aircraft designs in the United States underwent only few basic engineering changes until 1930, when the Air Corps ordered its first low-wing, all-metal planes—the General Aviation XA-7 and the Curtiss XA-8, both of which were delivered for tests in 1931. However, the XA-7 lost out in competition against the XA-8, which thus became the first airplane to break the tradition of biplanes.

The A-8 was meant to fill a gap in Army aviation.

Until the appearance of this plane all attack-bombers had been modifications of observation types and were therefore not truly specialized. The A-8 was designed strictly for low-level operations in support of ground troops.

During 1932 the Air Corps ordered 13 of the planes for testing, calling them YA-8 and Y1A-8. The designations were later changed to A-8. These all had the 600-horsepower Curtiss Conqueror in-line engine and maximum speed of about 184 miles per hour. The last Y1A-8 had an engine change, boosting the power to 675, but the speed was actually lowered because of increased weight.

With another engine change—this time to the Pratt & Whitney Hornet radial of 625 horsepower—the designation became A-10, though the airplane was basically unchanged. Further improvements, plus substitution of a Wright Cyclone engine, resulted in the A-12, which was the final model. Total production of all versions was only 60.

All models of the Shrike had four forward-firing .30-caliber machine guns in the landing gear fairings plus one swivel gun in the rear cockpit. Normal bomb load consisted of 400 pounds hung on wing racks and below the fuselage. Extra fuel could also be carried in a tank beneath the fuselage.

The Shrike was not truly successful as a military plane. It was slow, unwieldy, and had very limited capabilities. However, it more than earned its place in aviation history. It was not only the first all-metal, low-wing monoplane in service, but the first with an enclosed cockpit for the pilot and the first with wing flaps to reduce landing speed.

Other data (A-12): Wing span, 44 feet; length, 32 feet 3 inches; loaded weight, 5,745 pounds; engine, 690-horsepower Wright Cyclone; maximum speed, 177 miles per hour at sea level.

The A-12 was basically similar to the A-8, but with a Hornet radial engine instead of the Conqueror in-line.

The A-12 mounted four forward-firing guns and a single swivel gun. Its normal bomb load was only 400 pounds.

Boeing's XB-901 was the first military plane with an all-metal cantilever wing and twin engines in the wing.

Above: One Y1B-9 was fitted with 600-h.p. Conqueror engines for tests. Below: Five Y1B-9A's were ordered, with Pratt & Whitney radials. Top speed was 186 m.p.h.

BOEING B-9 DEATH ANGEL

In 1930 the Boeing Airplane Company designed a low-wing, all-metal, single-engined transport plane called the Model 200 Monomail. It was the first truly modern transport ever designed in the United States, and its performance was superior to any transport then flying anywhere in the world.

Boeing thought that a larger version of the Monomail, with twin engines, might be of interest to the Army Air Corps. The company was so sure of the success of its design that it started production without official approval from the military.

When the Model 214 was flown for the first time on April 29, 1931, it was far ahead of any bomber ever built. It was not only faster than most fighters, but it also had a retractable landing gear—the first used on any military airplane.

18

The Air Corps was so impressed with the machine that it bought the first model and designated it XB-901. On the flight from the Boeing factory at Seattle, Washington, to Wright Field in Dayton, Ohio, the plane averaged 158 miles per hour. Only two refueling stops were required during the flight.

While the XB-901 was under test, the Air Corps ordered another version with 600-horsepower Curtiss Conqueror in-line engines and five with Pratt & Whitney radials of similar power. The Conqueror engine version was designated Y1B-9, and those with Pratt & Whitney engines were Y1B-9A's.

The B-9 was a revolution in bombardment aviation, but it was not ordered into volume production because the Martin Company had developed a machine that was still better and faster (see page 20). Boeing had gambled and had lost. However, it had started a new trend in civil as well as military aviation.

Other data (Y1B-9A): Wing span, 76 feet; length, 51 feet 5 inches; loaded weight, 13,919 pounds; engines, two 600-horsepower Pratt & Whitney Hornets; maximum speed, 186 miles per hour at 6,000 feet.

A smooth Y1B-9A flying with an equally smooth P-26A fighter, both by Boeing and both advanced for their time.

The YB-10 was the first American bomber with an enclosed gun turret. The other crew stations were open.

Production models had enclosures for all three crew members. Normal bomb load consisted of 2,260 pounds.

MARTIN B-10 FLYING WHALE

While the Boeing B-9 (see page 18) was interesting as a project, it was unsuccessful as a design and was not ordered into production. The credit for designing the first modern, all-metal, monoplane bomber must go to the Martin Company.

The firm built its Model 123 as a private venture, hoping to get back into the bomber business. The Air Corps expressed interest and agreed to test it under the designation XB-907. The date was July, 1932. After evaluation, however, the machine was rejected for production. The main reason for this decision was that the landing speed was considered too fast—93 miles per hour instead of the 63 miles per hour demanded by the Air Corps.

But C.A. Van Dusen, Martin's General Manager, refused to accept defeat. He had the bomber flown back to the factory and put his engineers and craftsmen to work day and night.

During a 60-day period the factory rebuilt the wings, adding four feet. It also installed Wright Cyclone engines of higher horsepower than the original Pratt & Whitney Hornets, rebuilt the nose of the fuselage and installed for the first time on any airplane a completely enclosed gun turret, enclosed the pilot's and co-pilot's cockpits in transparent sliding canopies, rebuilt the landing gear retraction system, and made other alterations.

The extensively altered XB-907A was resubmitted to the Air Corps on October 7, 1932. In its new version the landing speed was lowered to the required 63 miles per hour. The military was excited about the big machine. It was purchased and given the designation XB-10.

A total of 163 planes was ordered in the series. One, the turbosupercharged YB-10A, had a maximum speed of 236 miles per hour at 25,000 feet.

The B-10 was considered to be such an outstanding accomplishment that in 1932 the Martin Company was awarded the Collier Trophy, aviation's highest award.

Two B-10's over San Antonio, Texas, in 1940, at which time the planes had been relegated to training duties.

The same airplane was sold to various foreign nations. Several of the 120 delivered to the Netherlands were still operating in the Pacific two years after the Japanese attack at Pearl Harbor in 1941. These sank 26 enemy ships, including a battleship.

Other data (B-10B): Wing span, 70 feet 6 inches; length, 44 feet 9 inches; loaded weight, 14,887 pounds; engines, two 700-horsepower Wright Cyclones; maximum speed, 215 miles per hour at 6,500 feet.

Final version of the plane was called the YB-12A. It had extra fuel tanks in the bomb bay for increased range.

NORTHROP A-17

The Northrop Corporation, under the leadership of John K. Northrop, was one of the most advanced aircraft manufacturers in the United States in the early 1930's. Instead of producing biplanes, as most firms were doing, Northrop concentrated its efforts on monoplanes. One of its early ventures was the six-passenger Alpha, the first American plane with an all-metal, stressed-skin monocoque fuselage. Next came the Beta, the Delta, the Gamma, and other all-metal monoplanes.

In 1933 the company used its Delta-Gamma configuration to produce an attack-bomber called the Model 2-C. The following year the plane was accepted by the Air Corps for tests and designated YA-13. This first version had a 710-horsepower Wright Cyclone engine. The plane was later fitted with a 950-horsepower Pratt & Whitney Twin Wasp. However, this engine was too powerful, and 110 models of the plane, with various changes, were ordered as A-17's, mounting 750-horsepower Twin Wasp Jr. radials.

A-17 production versions actually had only faint similarity to the original Model 2-C. The fuselage, tail, cockpits, and landing gear were all changed, and the tips of the wings were more rounded. Armament was four wing-mounted .30-caliber machine guns and one swivel gun in the rear cockpit.

In 1936 the plane was changed again. The land-ing gear was made to retract, and the engine was boosted to 825 horsepower. These alterations increased the maximum speed 17 miles per hour. The Air Corps ordered 129 A-17A's.

The A-17 was the first really successful Air Corps

This is Northrop's original Model 2-C, which had four wing-mounted guns. The plane was redesignated YA-13.

attack-bomber, and it remained in service through the early months of World War II. The final version of the plane was developed by Douglas, which had taken over Northrop, and was built as the A-33 in 1942.

Other data (A-17A): Wing span, 47 feet 8 inches; length, 31 feet 8 inches; loaded weight, 7,545 pounds; engine, 825-horsepower Pratt & Whitney Twin Wasp Jr.; maximum speed, 220 miles per hour at 2,500 feet.

Above: First production version was the A-17, which had a fixed landing gear. Maximum speed was 206 m.p.h.

Below: The improved A-17A had a retractable landing gear and other alterations which improved performance.

BOEING B-17 FLYING FORTRESS

If the Martin B-10 (see page 20) could be called outstanding, then the Boeing Model 299, which eventually became the B-17 Flying Fortress, must be considered nothing less than spectacular in the history of American bomber planes.

The machine was designed to meet an Air Corps request for a bomber to replace the B-10. The new airplane was required to carry a bomb load of 2,000 pounds for not less than 1,020 miles at a speed of not less than 200 miles per hour.

Boeing's answer was the Model 299, which was ready for testing on July 28, 1935. The machine was the largest landplane in the United States and the world's fastest bomber. It was also the most heavily armed, with five machine-gun stations. The bomb load was not 2,000 pounds but 4,800, and maximum speed was 236 miles per hour.

The Army was so impressed with the machine that 13 Y1B-17's were ordered in January, 1936. The first service models, B-17B's, were ordered in 1938. Only 13 of these had been delivered when World War II started in Europe in 1939.

The Air Corps had 47 B-17's in the Pacific area when the Japanese attacked on December 7, 1941. Many of these were destroyed on the ground. How-

Top: The Model 299 during its first roll-out from the Boeing factory. Center: A three-element flight of improved YB-17's. Lower: The B-17C was further improved.

ever, those that escaped became the first American aircraft to see offensive action in the war when on December 10 three of them bombed Japanese shipping.

B-17's were used in every theatre of operations. In Europe alone, Flying Fortresses dropped 640,036 tons of bombs. All other Allied bombers and fighters dropped a total of 463,000 tons of bombs. While their principal function was to carry the war to the enemy, B-17's performed many other tasks. They were used to drop guided bombs, lifeboats, and propaganda leaflets. A number of special versions, called YB-40's, were fitted with up to 30 machine guns and cannon and used as escorts to protect bomber formations.

By the end of the war, a total of 12,731 Flying Fortresses had been built—6,981 by Boeing, 2,750 by Lockheed, and 3,000 by Douglas. During its operational life the plane's speed was increased to 317 miles per hour in the B-17E and its bomb load was increased to 17,600 pounds in the final model, the B-17G.

Other data (B-17G): Wing span, 103 feet 9 inches; length, 74 feet 4 inches; loaded weight, 65,500 pounds; engines, four 1,200-horsepower Wright Cyclones; maximum speed, 287 miles per hour at 25,000 feet.

Top: A flight of B-17E's unloading bombs over a German target. Center: The B-17F had 13 .50-caliber machine guns. Lower: B-17G's had twin-gun chin turrets.

25

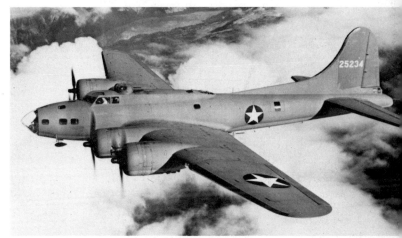

The B-18 was a military adaptation of the Douglas DC-2 transport. It was not a notable bomber in any respect.

DOUGLAS B-18 BOLO

The B-18, like the Boeing B-17, was originally submitted to the Air Corps as a replacement for the Martin B-10 (see page 20). The four-engined Boeing bomber was ready for testing in July, 1935, some two months before the B-18 was first flown at Wright Field. But while production of the Flying Fortress was delayed, except for a few service-test models, the B-18 was selected for immediate production, with a first order for 133.

The B-18, which was later named Bolo by the British Royal Air Force, was not actually a new design but was a military version of the famed Douglas DC-2 transport. There were a number of external changes, including a deeper fuselage for internal stowage of bombs, a new nose, and a longer wing span.

The Douglas bomber was a considerable im-

provement over the Martin B-10. It was larger and carried a much heavier bomb load in its final version, but its maximum speed was only 2 miles per hour faster and its cruising speed 26 miles per hour less.

Alterations were made in the B-18 design in 1937, and an additional 177 were ordered. The new model, the B-18A, had a new nose to give the bombardier better vision. There was also an engine change, providing an additional 140 horsepower total. Another 40 B-18A's were ordered in 1938, bringing over-all production of the series to 350. All versions had three gun positions, each with a single .30-caliber machine gun on a manual swivel.

In 1939 Douglas made a number of major alterations in the original design, changing the wing as well as the fuselage, and boosting the maximum speed to 282 miles per hour. The new plane was called the B-23 Dragon, and it was the first American bomber to have a tail gun. But while the B-23 had much better performance than the earlier versions, only 38 were produced.

The B-18 was the Air Corps' first-line bomber when the United States became involved in World War II. However, only few of them saw combat action, and with limited success.

Other data (B-18A): Wing span, 89 feet 6 inches; length, 57 feet 10 inches; loaded weight, 22,675 pounds; engines, two 1,000-horsepower Wright Cyclones; maximum speed, 218 miles per hour at 10,000 feet.

Above: The B-18A had a changed nose to give the bombardier better vision. Its speed was only 218 m.p.h.

Below: Final version of the series was the B-23 Dragon. It was the first U.S. bomber with a tail turret.

DOUGLAS A-20 HAVOC

The A-20 Havoc was produced in larger numbers than any other Air Force attack-bomber, the first American airplane to see action in World War II with U.S. crews, and the first American warplane to carry interception radar. But despite this record, the Havoc was not originally built for American forces and was not developed with encouragement from the American military.

As early as 1936 the engineers at Douglas Aircraft realized that the A-17 (see page 22) was already obsolete, and they decided to design a possible replacement. This was the Model 7B, which was completed in December, 1938.

At that time the French had an Air Commission in the United States to buy airplanes. They saw the 7B and ordered 105 with various changes. This resulted in the DB-7, the first model of which was completed on August 17, 1939.

When France was defeated by the Germans in May, 1940, the British took over the contract and made further improvements. Meanwhile, the Army Air Corps also ordered 123 A-20A's.

About 980 DB-7's were delivered to the Royal Air Force. The first of these made their initial

First version of the Havoc for U.S. forces was the A-20A. The plane became the most-produced attack-bomber.

The A-20G had eight machine guns and carried 2,600 pounds of bombs. This machine has an auxiliary belly tank.

attacks against the Germans on February 12, 1942. However, the Havoc was not used for combat by the Army Air Forces until July 4, 1942.

The most heavily-armed version was the A-20G, some of which mounted four 20-millimeter cannon and four .50-caliber machine guns. Most planes of this model had eight or nine .50-caliber guns. Underwing bomb racks in the A-20G also increased the bomb load from 2,600 pounds to 4,000 pounds.

In 1942 and 1943 a number of Havocs were converted to night fighters and called P-70 Midnight Maulers. These were equipped with radar and were used as interceptors.

The final version was the A-20K, which appeared in 1943. The 7,385th and last Havoc was rolled from the production line on September 20, 1944.

In 1945 Douglas Aircraft made a listing of the engineering hours required on the plane. Before the first model was ready for combat, it had consumed 481,662 engineering hours. By the time the plane went out of production, including 12 model versions, it had required 3,521,173 man-hours of engineering!

Other data (A-20K): Wing span, 61 feet 4 inches; length, 48 feet 4 inches; loaded weight, 27,000 pounds; engines, two 1,700-horsepower Wright Cyclones; maximum speed, 334 miles per hour at 15,600 feet.

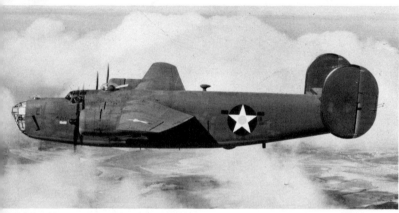

CONSOLIDATED B-24 LIBERATOR

The argument over which was the better plane, the Boeing B-17 Flying Fortress or the Consolidated B-24 Liberator, has been waged for many years among pilots and aviation historians. It is an argument which will continue indefinitely, since both sides are unshakable in their convictions.

The B-17's maximum speed was higher than that of the B-24, but the Liberator had a better cruising speed. It also had a longer range, a faster rate of climb, and the ability to carry a larger load of explosives over a short distance. The plane was a veritable flying battleship and was capable of absorbing tremendous amounts of damage.

Early in 1944 Peter Masefield, the noted British aviation writer, called the Liberator "one of the three most outstanding aircraft in the world." This was one man's opinion, but it is a fact that more Liberators were built than any other American airplane used in World War II—a total of 19,251 in all versions, including PB4Y-1's for the U.S. Navy.

The story of the B-24 began in January, 1939, when the Air Corps asked Consolidated to design a bomber with better performance than the Flying Fortress, which was then in production. The mili-

Top: The original XB-24 in 1939. Center: First large-scale production version was the B-24D. Lower: More B-24J's were produced than any other Liberator model.

The B-24M was the final production version. However, it was not notably improved over the previous models.

The single-tail XB-24N appeared in 1944. It was the last of the Liberators and only seven were produced.

tary wanted a machine with a cruising range of 3,000 miles, a maximum speed of more than 300 miles per hour, and a service ceiling of 35,000 feet.

Consolidated had already begun design studies on a four-engined heavy bomber prior to the Air Corps request. This was called the Model 32, and preliminary specifications were ready within three weeks after the military had approached the company. An experimental model was ordered on March 30, 1939.

The XB-24 was ready for flight testing on December 29, 1939. After a short test program, the Air Corps ordered seven YB-24's, followed by a production order for 36 B-24A's. All of these had hand-operated machine guns and a gross weight of 46,400 pounds, which was 5,400 pounds more than the XB-24.

Nine of the planes originally ordered as B-24A's

were delivered as B-24C's. These had power gun turrets on top of the fuselage and in the belly. There were also waist guns, nose guns, and tail guns on free swivels.

The first model ordered in quantity was the B-24D, which had a loaded weight of 56,000 pounds. However, the version produced in largest numbers was the B-24J. A total of 6,678 was built.

Liberators flew in every theatre of combat. Air Force models alone flew 312,734 sorties and dropped 634,831 tons of bombs. They also scored more victories over enemy fighters than any other type of bombing plane in service with the Allies.

Other data (B-24J): Wing span, 110 feet; length, 67 feet 2 inches; loaded weight, 65,000 pounds; engines, four 1,200-horsepower Pratt & Whitney Twin Wasps; maximum speed, 294 miles per hour at 25,000 feet.

This is the original NA-40, which did not receive a military designation. It was destroyed during testing.

Second version of the plane was called NA-62. It was almost an entirely new design, with a tail gun added.

NORTH AMERICAN B-25 MITCHELL

Many American airplanes won fame and their place in aeronautical history during World War II, but none of these achieved a more outstanding record than the B-25 Mitchell, which has been called one of the most versatile planes of the war.

Despite its impressive combat record, the design got off to a very inauspicious start. The machine was designed in 1938 to meet an Air Corps require-ment for a medium bomber. The original plane, the North American NA-40, was completed and first flown in January, 1939. It mounted two 1,100-horsepower Pratt & Whitney Wasps, but these were soon changed for 1,350-horsepower Wright Cyclones. This first test model was delivered to the Army in March, 1939. Two weeks later it was destroyed in a crash.

North American was asked to build another version of the plane, with a number of changes. This

The Air Corps ordered 184 B-25's. These were basically similar to the NA-62, with a number of minor changes.

Armament was increased on the B-25B. The tail gun was eliminated, but twin-gunned power turrets were added.

was not ready for testing until August 19, 1940; however, 184 service models had already been ordered.

The Mitchell made news for the first time on April 18, 1942, when 16 of the machines under the leadership of Lieutenant Colonel James Doolittle took off from the aircraft carrier *Hornet* and carried out the first air attacks against Japan. All of the planes were lost and most of the crew members captured, but an important psychological blow had been struck.

In 1942 a B-25C was modified to carry a 75-millimeter cannon in its nose and designated B-25G. This was the largest gun ever mounted on an airplane during the war, and 300 B-25G's were produced. This was followed by the B-25H, which was the most heavily armed airplane of the war. In addition to the cannon, it had 14 .50-caliber guns. This version was used against enemy shipping and for ground strafing.

The next and final model, the B-25J, was without the cannon but had 12 machine guns. It was also the most-produced model. A total of almost 11,000 Mitchells was built, 4,318 of which were B-25J's. The last of these were not retired from service until January, 1959.

Other data (B-25J): Wing span, 67 feet 7 inches; length, 52 feet 11 inches; loaded weight, 35,000 pounds; engines, two 1,700-horsepower Wright Cyclones; maximum speed, 275 miles per hour at 13,000 feet.

Above: The B-25C and D models were identical but were built by different factories. Below: The B-25H was a flying battleship, with 14 machine guns plus a cannon.

DOUGLAS A-24 BANSHEE

The Douglas A-24 had a truly strange history. In 1933 Northrop developed its Model 2-C, which finally became the A-17 (see page 22). Around this same time the firm also produced the BT-1 for the U.S. Navy. This plane was not actually a new design, but an altered and improved version of the A-17.

One of the 54 production BT-1's was changed again, becoming the XBT-2. By this time, however, Northrop was taken over by Douglas as the Douglas El Segundo Division, and the designation of the ordered BT-2's was changed by the Navy to SBD-1 Dauntless. Production versions started reaching Marine Corps squadrons late in 1940.

World War II had broken out in Europe, and the German Junkers Ju.87 Stuka had become the scourge of the skies. However, the Air Force did not have a dive-bomber worthy of the name, and

Above: The first A-24's were similar to Navy versions, with deck hook removed. Left: A flight of A-24's. The slow planes were obsolete before they were delivered.

it ordered 78 A-24's from Douglas. The need for these was considered so urgent that the planes actually delivered were diverted from the Navy production line and were identical to the SBD-3's except that the deck hook for carrier landings was removed. The first Banshees were delivered to the Air Force in 1941.

Less than a month after the first contract for A-24's was completed, the planes were sent to the Pacific area to strengthen American defensive positions. When the A-24's went into combat, however,

they were found to be too slow, too vulnerable to attack, and vastly underarmed. Normal armament consisted of only two .50-caliber guns on the engine cowl synchronized to fire through the propeller arc and two .30-caliber guns in the rear cockpit. Their range of only 1,200 miles was also too short for effective operations. According to an Air Force statement made much later, the planes were virtually "clay pigeons" for Japanese fighters.

But while the A-24's were slow and vulnerable, more advanced replacements were slow in coming off the production lines and combat aircraft were desperately needed. This need resulted in contracts for an additional 170 A-24A's in 1942 and 615 A-24B's the following year.

It is ironic that while the A-24 was not successful with the Air Force, the same airplane served the Navy with distinction. Combat records reveal that the Dauntless was flown into action more often than any other carrier-based bomber, had the lowest ratio of losses, and sank a larger tonnage of enemy warships than any other Navy aircraft. The crew of one SBD was also credited with shooting down seven enemy airplanes in only two days.

Other data (A-24B): Wing span, 41 feet 6 inches; length, 32 feet 8 inches; loaded weight, 9,200 pounds; engine, 1,200-horsepower Wright Cyclone; maximum speed, 252 miles per hour at 17,502 feet.

In attacking attitude, with dive flaps lowered. Air Force experience with A-24 Banshees was disappointing.

This is the first B-26, three days after flight testing. It was then the fastest bomber in the Air Corps.

The B-26B was built in largest numbers. Bomb load was 3,000 pounds, and it had six defensive machine guns.

MARTIN B-26 MARAUDER

There has never been another airplane with a record like that of the Marauder. The crews either loved it or hated it, they either swore by it or at it, they called it a pilot-killer or the safest of all warplanes. Mention the B-26 at any gathering of World War II pilots, and it always develops into an argument. No other airplane in the annals of warfare has evoked contradictory emotions as thoroughly as the B-26.

Cold statistics prove beyond question, however, that the Marauder was one of the greatest bombers ever built. Its loss in combat was less than one-half of 1 per cent—the lowest of any Allied bomber in the war. More than 250 B-26's completed 100 missions each. One of these, *Flak Bait*, was the first Allied bomber to complete 100 missions, and

the first to complete 200 missions. Marauders flew more than 110,000 sorties during the war and dropped in excess of 150,000 tons of bombs.

The B-26 was evolved as a result of an Air Corps request for a medium bomber in January, 1939. The military was seeking a bomber with high speed characteristics while carrying a minimum load of 2,000 pounds of bombs. Six months later the Glenn L. Martin Company submitted its design project, the Model 179.

The Air Corps ordered the new bomber into production without waiting for a test model. The first contract called for 1,100 planes, to be delivered as rapidly as possible. Before the design was finally phased out, a total of 5,266 was built.

The first B-26 was ready for testing on November 25, 1940. At that time the plane was called the Flying Torpedo, because of the streamlined shape of its body, and in anticipation of further contracts, the company tooled up for mass production.

Flight tests proved that the Marauder was even faster than the Air Corps had requested. It also carried a heavier bomb load than specified—5,800 pounds. But to meet the speed requirements, it had the highest wing loading of any plane delivered for service, thus resulting in a very high landing speed.

B-26's saw their first action in April, 1942, in an attack against Japanese positions in New Guinea. Two months later they were used as torpedo-bombers during the Battle of Midway. They saw combat in Europe for the first time on May 14, 1943, when 11 of the planes struck an electricity generating plant in Holland. Not one Marauder returned from this raid. In time, however, the Air Force realized that the plane required only the very best of pilots to ride it through safely. Following this, the Marauder became the best tactical bomber of the war, with the best safety record.

Other data (B-26G): Wing span, 71 feet; length, 58 feet 6 inches; loaded weight, 37,000 pounds; engines, two 2,000-horsepower Pratt & Whitney Double Wasps; maximum speed, 323 miles per hour at 5,000 feet.

Top: A B-26C and Republic Thunderbolt over France after a bombing raid. Center: A B-26F in invasion colors dropping bombs. Lower: Last model was the B-26G.

The last of three XB-29's during a test flight. The plane was an entirely new concept in aerial weapons.

BOEING B-29 SUPERFORTRESS

In 1940 the Army Air Corps realized that it would need a very heavy long-range bomber in the event that the United States was drawn into the war that had begun in Europe, and various aircraft companies were requested to submit proposals and bids. On the strength of its earlier experience with the huge XB-15 (first flown on October 15, 1937), the Boeing Airplane Company designed its Model 345. The Air Corps studied plans submitted by several firms, judged the Boeing design best, and ordered three planes under the designation XB-29.

Before construction was begun on the first experimental model, the Superfortress went through eight major design changes. These modifications resulted in an increase in range from 4,000 miles to almost 6,000 miles. The top speed was also raised from 248 to 363 miles per hour, and the maximum bomb load was increased from 5,800 to 20,000

pounds. More aerodynamic research and testing was conducted to develop the B-29 than any previous airplane built by Boeing.

The first XB-29 was ready for flight testing on September 21, 1941. Even before this machine was completed, however, another 1,514 had been ordered.

Though huge, the Superfortress was faster than most single-seat fighters. It had heavy defensive armament.

B-29's were not used in the European Theatre. They were flown exclusively against the Japanese, and they dropped a total of 171,060 tons of bombs on our Asian enemy compared to 6,781 tons by all other aircraft. B-29's also carried the only atomic bombs ever dropped in warfare. The first of these fell on Hiroshima on August 6, 1945, and the second was dropped on Nagasaki three days later. As a direct result of these raids, Japan surrendered

As with other Superfortresses, the B-29B had five gun turrets and two bomb bays carrying up to 20,000 pounds.

on August 14.

A total of 3,970 B-29's was built—2,766 by Boeing, 668 by Bell, and 536 by Martin. On November 25, 1945, a B-29 called the *Pacusan Dreamboat* set a new nonstop, nonrefueling record by flying from the island of Guam in the Pacific to Washington, D.C., a distance of 8,189 miles. The same airplane later raised the distance record to 9,500 miles.

The B-29 Superfortress was more than just another large bomber; it was actually a new concept in aerial weapons. It was the first bomber put in production with an altitude-conditioned fuselage, and the first with a remote gun aiming and firing system. Normal armament consisted of up to 13 machine guns or a combination of machine guns and cannon.

Other data (B-29B): Wing span, 141 feet 3 inches; length, 99 feet; loaded weight, 137,500 pounds; engines, four 2,200-horsepower Wright Cyclones; maximum speed, 368 miles per hour at 25,000 feet.

CURTISS A-25 HELLDIVER

The Curtiss Company designed and built a long series of light bombers for the Air Corps and Navy called Falcons and Helldivers. The last Navy biplane Helldiver, the SBC-4, was put into production in 1936. Three years later, while the SBC-4 was still in production, the Navy requested various manufacturers to submit bids for a new scout-bomber with improved performance characteristics.

One of the planes entered in the competition was the XSB2C-1, the last Curtiss design to carry the name Helldiver. The test model was first flown on December 18, 1940. However, production versions were drastically altered, with 889 major changes and hundreds of minor changes. These improvements resulted in an airplane which both American and British experts called "the world's best dive-bomber."

In 1941 the Air Force also ordered 900 Helldivers, calling them A-25A's. These were similar to the Navy SB2C-1's, though with the deck hook and wing-folding mechanism removed as well as other minor changes for land-based operations.

In Navy service, the SB2C was an important weapon and scored heavily against the Japanese

Three views of the A-25 Helldiver. The plane was basically similar to the Navy's SB2C-1, though with various minor alterations for operations from land bases.

The Helldiver was called "the world's best dive-bomber," but it was used only in small numbers by the Air Force.

at Rabaul, in the Marshall Islands, and elsewhere. In one raid alone the planes were credited with sinking an enemy light cruiser and a destroyer, a heavy cruiser probably sunk, and a light cruiser heavily damaged.

But despite the success of the Helldiver in the Pacific area, the Air Force used the plane only in limited numbers and turned the remainder of its A-25A's over to the Marine Corps, which designated them as SB2C-1A's.

Other data: Wing span, 49 feet 9 inches; length, 36 feet 8 inches; loaded weight, 16,000 pounds; engine, 1,700-horsepower Wright Cyclone; maximum speed, 275 miles per hour at 15,000 feet.

DOUGLAS A-26 INVADER

The A-26 was the last important attack-bomber ordered by the Air Force for service in World War II. It was called "the most versatile, as well as the fastest, American-built attack-bomber." This was an understatement, for the plane was actually the fastest of all attack-bombers in service with the Allies except for short bursts of speed. In 1944, during a normal ferrying flight, an A-26, *The Duckfoot Sue,* had a race of 1,000 miles with a De Havilland Mosquito, the fastest British attack plane, and won by 20 minutes.

As early as 1940 the Air Corps realized that its standard attack-bombers, as well as those under development, would require replacement with more advanced designs. This resulted in a bid which went out to various manufacturers. The Douglas proposal appeared to be the best, and three experimental models were ordered in 1941. These were the XA-26, a light bombardment attack plane; the XA-26A, a modification to be used as a night fighter; and the XA-26B, which had heavy armament—including a 75-millimeter cannon—for destroyer-type work. The first of these, the XA-26, was ready for tests on July 10, 1942.

The plane was an instant success and was ordered into immediate production. Actually, the XA-26 carried approximately twice the bomb load required by the original specifications.

Invaders saw combat for the first time on November 19, 1944, when they struck targets in Brest and Metz, France, flying from bases in England. In their first 17 missions, only one A-26 was lost.

The A-26 was one of the safest warplanes ever

Early models of the Invader did not have belly guns, depending on speed for defense against enemy fighters.

With six .50-caliber guns in the nose, plus a two-gun top turret, the A-26B had heavy attacking firepower.

A three-element flight of A-26's. Note two-gun belly turret. The plane could carry 4,000 pounds of bombs.

built. This was due not only to its high speed, but also its rugged construction. According to the Air Force, it was also more accurate in striking targets because of its inherent stability.

"One Invader came back with a four-inch flak hole in one aileron and flak holes all over the fuselage," according to Dom Mercurio, a Douglas service man in England. "A lot of them came back with only one engine," he added.

The Invader was built in models A-26B and A-26C. Contracts for more than 4,500 were canceled after Japan surrendered. However, many of the planes, redesignated B-26's, were used in Korea. They also dropped the last bombs of that war.

Other data (A-26C): Wing span, 70 feet; length, 51 feet 3 inches; loaded weight, 40,000 pounds; engines, two 2,000-horsepower Pratt & Whitney Double Wasps; maximum speed, 373 miles per hour at sea level.

An A-26C with two Ryan Firebees under its wings. With these missiles, targets could be hit from long range.

LOCKHEED A-29 HUDSON

In 1936 the Lockheed Aircraft Corporation introduced a beautiful twin-engined, low-wing transport called the Electra. It carried six passengers and had a cruising speed of about 200 miles per hour. The following year—July 29, 1937—a larger version of the machine took off from Burbank, California, for its first flight. It was called the Model 14 Super Electra, and it was designed as a 14-passenger commercial transport. The plane was destined to win fame but as a medium bomber.

The British started the design on its way to history when in June, 1938, they ordered 250 altered versions as bombers for the Royal Air Force, calling them Hudsons.

The Hudson became almost legendary with the Royal Air Force. It was the first airplane delivered from the U.S. to Europe by air, it was the first American airplane to fight in World War II, the first airplane in history to capture a submarine, and the first to sink a submarine.

While the first Hudson bombers were built for the British, they were also given an Air Corps

Though originally a commercial transport, the Hudson won wartime fame with both the R.A.F. and U.S. Air Force.

With the addition of a twin-gun dorsal turret, the Hudson was designated AT-18 and used for training gunners.

designation, A-28. The plane was later improved, with more powerful engines, and these were called A-29's. As with the original Hudsons, the A-29's were also ordered by the British, but a number were later repossessed by the Air Force. One of these was the first Air Force plane credited with a successful attack on a German submarine.

At best, the Hudson was poorly armed and had only acceptable performance. Normal armament was five .30-caliber guns, and the bomb load for average missions was 1,600 pounds. Cruising speed under ideal conditions was 205 miles per hour. But despite its drawbacks, the Hudson has gone down in history as one of the most successful airplanes of World War II. Crew members often referred to it as "Old Boomerang," because the plane always seemed to come back from missions, though badly battered by enemy ground fire or fighters.

Other data: Wing span, 65 feet 6 inches; length, 44 feet 3 inches; loaded weight, 20,500 pounds; engines, two 1,200-horsepower Wright Cyclones; maximum speed, 254 miles per hour at 15,000 feet.

Above: An A-31 with dive flaps extended. Below: Note distinctive wing, making the plane easy to identify.

VULTEE A-31 VENGEANCE

The Vultee Vengeance became an unfortunate casualty of changing concepts of warfare, for it was a far better fighting machine than its combat record would indicate.

When the British Purchasing Commission visited the United States in 1940, one of its purposes was to locate a counterpart to the German Junkers Ju.87 Stuka dive-bomber. Several proposals were inspected, and the Vultee V-72 seemed to be the best and a contract was awarded for a limited number.

The first Royal Air Force Vengeance was ready in July, 1941. After tests, the British called for various alterations and ordered 700 duplicates.

The first production airplane was completed in June, 1942. By this time, however, experience in warfare proved that the dive-bomber was virtually a sitting target unless it operated with strong fighter cover or in areas where aerial superiority had been established. The R.A.F. therefore transferred its Vengeance dive-bombers to Burma, where they proved highly effective.

Meanwhile, the U.S. Army Air Force also ordered 300 of the planes, calling them A-31's. Some 240 of those originally ordered by the British were also taken over by the United States when this country was drawn into the war.

The A-31's had six forward-firing .30-caliber guns and two swivel guns. When .50-caliber guns were substituted, the designation was changed to A-35A. With an engine change, boosting the output by 100 horsepower, the plane was called the A-35B.

By this time dive-bombers were almost obsolete as weapons, and only a few of the Vultees saw combat, most of them being used for target towing.

Other data (A-35B): Wing span, 48 feet; length, 39 feet 9 inches; loaded weight, 16,400 pounds; engine, 1,700-horsepower Wright Double Cyclone; maximum speed, 279 miles per hour at 13,500 feet.

The A-35 was equipped to full Air Force standards. It had four .50's firing forward and one rear swivel gun.

The Convair XB-32 appeared to be an enlarged B-24. It was the first bomber to have a pressurized fuselage.

CONVAIR B-32 DOMINATOR

Shortly after Boeing received an order to build three XB-29's in September, 1940, Consolidated was also contracted to produce three experimental XB-32's. The designs and assumed performance characteristics submitted by Boeing had appeared better than those of the other competitors (including Lockheed and Douglas as well as Consolidated), but this did not mean that the final aircraft would be better. The Air Force also wanted a backup bomber in case the Boeing did not prove completely successful, or if they were not able to

produce rapidly enough to meet unexpected combat demands.

The first XB-32 was ready for flight testing on September 7, 1942—exactly two weeks ahead of the XB-29. In general appearance, the plane seemed to be an enlarged B-24 Liberator, with the same wing and a similar tail. However, the fuselage was entirely different, and it was the first pressurized bomber for crew comfort at high altitudes.

Flight tests proved that the Dominator was faster than the Superfortress, but it was much smaller and carried a considerably smaller bomb load. As a result, the Air Force favored the B-29.

Even though it was considered second choice, 300 Dominators were ordered. However, the plane was almost completely redesigned from the XB-32. Major changes were made in the fuselage and empennage as well as in engines and wings. These changes saved 1,000 pounds of weight in the wing alone. It was also decided to give the plane a single huge tail in place of the twin tail on the first XB-32. This resulted in increased stability.

A total of 1,732 B-32's was ordered, but only 114 were produced and the remainder canceled because of lack of need. A mere 15 of the planes were used in combat before the Japanese surrendered.

Other data: Wing span, 135 feet; length, 82 feet 1 inch; loaded weight, 111,500 pounds; engines; four 2,200-horsepower Wright Cyclones; maximum speed, 358 miles per hour at 30,000 feet.

Above: Production versions had single tails. Only 114 of the planes were produced and 1,588 others canceled.

Below: The Dominator saw only limited combat action, but it was considered to be a successful development.

The XB-36 in flight with a Liberator. The B-36 fuselage length was two and a half times that of the Liberator.

CONVAIR B-36 PEACEMAKER

In April, 1941, when most of Europe had fallen to the German armies and the survival of England seemed doubtful, the Air Corps issued specifications for a bomber with performance capabilities which at the time were considered little short of fantastic. The specifications called for a machine capable of flying from the United States to targets 5,000 miles away and then returning without refueling.

Of the four designs submitted, the Consolidated Model 37 was selected, and two test versions were ordered. Shortly thereafter, Consolidated merged with Vultee, and the company name was changed to Consolidated-Vultee and then Convair. Still later it became the Convair Division of General Dynamics.

Because of the pressing need for B-24's, work on the XB-36 proceeded slowly, and the first plane was not rolled out until August 8, 1946. The second test model was the YB-36, later designated YB-36A.

While the B-36 was too late for World War II, it was called "the mightiest bomber ever built" and was credited with preventing the Russians from launching another global holocaust during the Cold War period.

A total of 385 B-36's in all versions was delivered. The plane was not only huge, with a wing 7 feet 6 inches thick at its deepest point, but it was faster than many World War II fighters. Original specifications had called for a bomb load of 72,000 pounds, but it was actually able to carry more than 84,000 pounds.

The final version, the YB-60, had a swept wing and eight jet engines. However, it was not ordered into production.

Other data (B-36J): Wing span, 230 feet; length, 162 feet 1 inch; loaded weight, 410,000 pounds; engines, six 3,800-horsepower Pratt & Whitney Wasp Majors and four 5,200-pounds-thrust General Electric turbojets; maximum speed, 435 miles per hour.

Top: First of 22 production B-36A's. Note bubble-type pilot enclosure. Center: The B-36D had four jet engines added. Lower: Final version was the YB-60 jet.

BOEING B-50 SUPERFORTRESS

In 1944 one B-29A (see page 38) had a number of major alterations and was redesignated XB-44. Among other changes, it was fitted with 3,500-horsepower Pratt & Whitney Wasp Major

Above: First experimental model for the B-50 was designated XB-44. Below: While the B-50A appeared identical to the B-29, it was actually 75 per cent new.

engines in place of the original 2,200-horsepower Wright Cyclones. The plane thus had vastly increased performance. Sixty were ordered as B-29D's, a designation later changed to B-50.

The new bomber was quite similar in appearance to the B-29. However, only 25 per cent of the original design and equipment was used. One of the few external alterations was to increase the height of the vertical tail section by some 5 feet.

The first B-50A was taken up for its initial tests on June 25, 1947. After 79 B-50A's had been built, these were followed by the B-50B, which had a loaded weight increase of 30,000 pounds. Next came the B-50D, with fuel tanks on wing pods.

In 1949 a B-50A, *Lucky Lady II*, made history when it completed the first nonstop flight around the world. During the 23,452-mile flight the plane was refueled in the air four times. Leaving Fort

The *Lucky Lady II* just taking off on the start of its historic 23,452-mile nonstop flight around the world.

Worth, Texas, on February 26, it was refueled over the Azores, Saudi Arabia, the Philippines, and the Hawaiian Islands. *Lucky Lady II* returned to Fort Worth on March 4, having spent 94 hours and one minute in the air at an average speed of more than 249 miles per hour.

A comparison of the B-29 and B-50 indicates the increase in bomber size during the period. In 1944 the B-29 was designated as a "very heavy bomber." It was also the largest bomber in service with the Air Force. Only nine years later the B-50, which weighed some 35,000 pounds more than the B-29, was officially called a medium bomber.

The B-50 was the first new bomber built for the Strategic Air Command following World War II. It also became the largest training plane ever produced when 24 of the planes, with no armament, were ordered as TB-50H's to train crews for the huge Convair B-36 (see page 50).

Other data (B-50D): Wing span, 141 feet 3 inches; length, 99 feet; loaded weight, 173,000 pounds; engines, four 3,500-horsepower Pratt & Whitney Wasp Majors; maximum speed, 445 miles per hour at 17,000 feet.

Above: An RB-50B reconnaissance version, with extra wing tanks carrying 700 gallons each. Below: A KB-50 is shown refueling three different planes at one time.

First production versions of the Tornado were designated B-45A. They were faster than most Air Force fighters.

NORTH AMERICAN B-45 TORNADO

The B-45 Tornado earned its place in aeronautical history as the first jet bomber ordered into production for the U.S. Air Force. It was also the world's first bomber to exceed the speed of 500 miles per hour. The only Air Force fighter capable of matching its speed was the Lockheed P-80 Shooting Star.

Only 142 Tornados were built in all versions. However, the plane was far more successful as a design than its production record indicates. The biggest difficulty with the B-45 was that it was a conventional design with jet power added. In other words, it had nothing new except its engines. But the plane was designed before the United States realized that swept wings were necessary to take full advantage of this new means of propulsion. It was thus the Tornado's plight to be caught in a transition period.

The B-45 was actually a giant step forward in bombardment aircraft. It had a wing span of some 32 feet less than that of the Boeing B-50 and an empty weight of about 32,000 pounds less—but it carried a larger bomb load, had a higher ceiling, and was about 200 miles per hour faster.

Design work on the plane began in 1944, when the Air Force asked North American to develop a jet bomber. The following year three experimental models were ordered for tests. Before the first XB-45 was taken up for its initial flight on March 17, 1947, a production contract for 96 B-45A's was issued.

The B-45A's, like the XB-45's, had four General Electric turbojets rated at 4,000-pounds-thrust. These did not give the desired performance, and engine power was increased to 5,200 pounds thrust in the next production model, the B-45C. This version had its loaded weight increased from 90,000 to 110,000 pounds and also had wing-tip fuel tanks with a capacity of 1,200 gallons, to increase the range.

After ten B-45C's had been completed, the plane was altered for photo-reconnaissance duties and designated RB-45C. This version mounted nine cameras pointing downward at various angles. The bomb bay was retained, but was redesigned to carry photo flash bombs and extra fuel tanks. The last RC-45C was delivered in October, 1951, after which the plane was phased out as more advanced designs were available.

Other data (B-45C): Wing span, 89 feet; length, 75 feet 5 inches; loaded weight, 112,955 pounds; engines, four 5,200-pounds-thrust General Electric turbojets; maximum speed, 580 miles per hour at sea level.

Left: The B-45C had wing-tip fuel tanks to increase the normal cruising range. Below: The RB-45C was the fastest version, with an all-out speed of 570 m.p.h.

Boeing's XB-47 was the first swept-wing bomber. During an early test it flew 2,289 miles at 607.2 m.p.h.

Only 10 B-47A's were built. Armament was two 12.7-mm. machine guns in the remotely-controlled tail position.

BOEING B-47 STRATOJET

The B-47 was the first jet bomber with a swept-back wing. It was also the world's first bomber to exceed 600 miles per hour in level flight.

As early as 1943 the Army Air Force realized that a jet bomber would be required, and requests were sent out to various manufacturers to submit bids. Boeing's first design to meet the desired specifications was their Model 424, which was submitted in March, 1944. This was similar to the B-29, with four jet engines. It was not approved. Next came the Model 432, another conventional design with four jets.

With the end of the war in Europe, Boeing engineers had an opportunity to study German research with swept wings. Plans for the Model 432 were immediately discarded and replaced by the Model 448, which had its wings swept back 35 degrees. It was to have four engines in the forward fuselage

and two in the rear. This was September, 1945. A month later the design was changed again to the Model 450, which finally became the Stratojet.

The Air Force ordered two XB-47's in June, 1946. The first of these was ready to fly on December 17, 1947—40 years to the day after the Wright brothers' first flight at Kitty Hawk, North Carolina.

In September, 1948, following an exhaustive test program, the Air Force ordered ten B-47A's. These had a loaded weight of 160,000 pounds—35,000 pounds more than the experimental models—and more powerful engines. The first XB-47, with the new engines, demonstrated its capabilities on February 8, 1949, when it established a new nonstop record of 2,289 miles in 3 hours and 46 minutes at an average speed of 607.2 miles per hour.

Next in the development program was the B-47B, 87 of which were originally ordered. This model had engines with 5,800 pounds thrust, an increase

Performance was improved in the B-47B. It could also carry 1,500-gallon wing fuel tanks for longer range.

Above: The RB-47E had cameras in the bomb bay. Below: The machine used jet- or rocket-assist for take-offs.

per engine of 600 pounds thrust, and the loaded weight was increased to 200,000 pounds. In 1950, as result of the Korean War, another 226 B-47B's were ordered.

The third model of the plane, the B-47C, was to have six engines rated at 9,400-pounds-thrust each. However, it was not put into production. Next in line was the XB-47D, with two turboprop engines and two turbojets. Two of these were built for tests but no others were ordered.

Final production model of the Stratojet was the B-47E. One of these established a speed record by averaging 794 miles per hour for 30 minutes, and another covered a nonstop distance of 39,200 miles in 80 hours and 36 minutes.

Other data (B-47E): Wing span, 116 feet; length, 109 feet 10 inches; loaded weight, 206,700 pounds; engines, six 6,000-pounds-thrust General Electric turbojets; maximum speed, 606 miles per hour at 16,300 feet.

The YB-52 was the first Stratofortress to fly. It was faster than any fighter in Air Force squadron service.

Only three B-52A's were built. Tests with these indicated that the plane required a number of alterations.

BOEING B-52 STRATOFORTRESS

The B-52 was one of the most important aerial weapons ever developed in the United States. It also remained in service longer than any bomber in history.

The story of the B-52 began in January, 1946, when the Air Force set up basic requirements for a new bomber with global capabilities and a large bomb capacity. Six months later Boeing was awarded an engineering study contract. After another two years, the firm was requested to build two test models, one designated XB-52 and the other YB-52. The XB-52 was completed in November, 1951, but was sent back to the factory for changes and was not flown until October 2, 1952. Meanwhile, the YB-52 was taken up for its first flight on April 15, 1952.

The first order for B-52A's was small—only 13 planes—because the Air Force considered the Stratofortress competitive with the unfinished Convair B-60, a jet powered development of the B-36 (see page 50). Only three B-52A's were actually built, followed by 50 improved B-52B's.

Meanwhile, the airplane was proving its amazing abilities. On September 4, 1954, the YB-52 was flown from Seattle, Washington, to the National Aircraft Show at Dayton, Ohio, at an average speed of 624 miles per hour—which was faster than the jet fighters in the Bendix Trophy Race that year.

Through the years B-52's toppled record after record. In January, 1957, three Stratofortresses flew nonstop around the world with mid-air refueling, averaging 530 miles per hour for the distance of

24,325 miles. Later the same year, six of the huge planes were flown nonstop from the United States to Argentina and back—10,425 miles without refueling. Still another record flight without refueling was 12,519 miles from Okinawa to Spain.

The 744th and last Stratofortress—a B-52H—was rolled off the Boeing assembly line at Wichita, Kansas, on June 22, 1962, thus ending a production life of 11 years. By previous military standards, the airplane should have been considered obsolete at that time. However, the B-52 still remained the best heavy bomber anywhere in the world.

Other data (B-52H): Wing span, 185 feet; length, 157 feet 7 inches; loaded weight, 480,000 pounds; engines, eight 17,000-pounds-thrust Pratt & Whitney turbojets; maximum speed, more than 660 miles per hour at 20,000 feet.

Top: B-52D's were heavier and more powerful than previous models. Center: A B-52E at take-off, flaps still down. Below: Contrails track a B-52G at high altitude.

A Hustler burning rubber at landing, its nose still high. The machine could fly twice the speed of sound.

CONVAIR B-58 HUSTLER

The B-58 was one of the most extraordinary airplanes ever built. It was developed as the world's first supersonic bomber and was capable of striking targets anywhere in the world with mid-air refueling, flying at a speed and altitude which few fighter planes could match.

But this was only part of the picture of the Hustler. The plane achieved a greater speed increase over the fastest previous strategic bomber than was realized in the preceding 50 years of aircraft design, and at dash speed it was more than twice as fast as any existing bomber.

Design studies for the B-58 started in 1949, and a contract for the plane was finally placed by the Air Force in August, 1952. The first model was completed on November 11, 1956, which was just two years and two months from the day the engineering drawings were released to the Convair manufacturing department. At roll-out, the plane was a sensation. It was the first bomber with a delta wing, the first with an area-rule or "Coke-bottle" fuselage, and the first to carry extra fuel or a bomb load, or both, in a disposable pod below the fuselage.

The disposable pod was a unique concept. The Convair engineers had reasoned that it was unnecessary for a bomber to carry useless empty space after its explosive load had been dropped, and so they designed the Hustler without a bomb bay as such. The machine was all airplane, with no empty space, and the pod was both fuel tank and bomb bay, to be disposed of when empty. In addition to the free-fall bomb pod, the B-58 could be fitted with a rocket-powered pod for launching far from the target, or with pods filled with reconnaissance or electronic countermeasure equipment.

The Air Force set six new records with the B-58 on January 13, 1961. One of these was a speed dash over 1,000 kilometers (about 621 miles) at 1,200.10 miles per hour. The plane also set a record of 1,061.81 miles per hour over 1,242 miles. On May 10, 1961, the Hustler set another record—1,302 miles per hour in a flight lasting more than half an hour.

Despite these records, Air Force test pilots said the B-58 had never been flown to its maximum speed, for fear that its wings and body would melt because of friction-induced heat!

Other data (B-58A): Wing span, 56 feet 10 inches; length, 96 feet 9 inches; loaded weight, more than 160,000 pounds; engines, four 10,000-pounds-thrust General Electric turbojets; maximum speed, 1,385 miles per hour at 40,000 feet.

Right: This photograph gives an excellent view of the bomber's unique delta wing. Below: The trim B-58 deploys a tail parachute to slow its hot landing roll.

The Air Force ordered 145 RB-66B's for photo-reconnaissance. The plane was adapted from the Navy's Skywarrior.

DOUGLAS B-66 DESTROYER

Following World War II the U.S. Navy realized that its aircraft carriers were far too small and that much larger carriers would have to be built. As the first of these giant carriers entered the planning stage, requests also went out to aircraft firms for a large carrier-borne bomber.

In 1949 Douglas was awarded a contract to produce two test models of the XA3D-1 Skywarrior, the largest and heaviest bomber for carrier operations. The first plane was ready for testing on October 28, 1952.

Meanwhile, the Air Force also ordered the plane under the designation RB-66A—for photo-reconnaissance duties rather than bombing. The first of five RB-66A's was ready for testing on June 28, 1954. The first true production model was called the RB-66B, 145 of which were built.

The function of the RB-66 was night photography. Flash bombs were carried in the bomb bay, and these were to illuminate an area while cameras in the plane photographed enemy installations.

The same basic design was also ordered as a bomber, and the first of 144 B-66B's was completed on January 4, 1956. The plane was designed to permit a wide selection of bomb combinations. It was also capable of carrying a hydrogen bomb.

Next came the RB-66C, which was for electronic reconnaissance. This was followed by the WB-66D, which was for electronic reconnaissance to obtain accurate weather information in combat areas.

All versions of the Destroyer were subsonic, but they were able to maintain high speeds over long distances. Two RB-66B's flown from Tucson, Arizona, to Eglin Air Force Base, Florida, averaged 700 miles per hour for the distance.

All models of the B-66 carried two 20-millimeter radar-controlled guns in the tail turret.

Other data (B-66B): Wing span, 72 feet 6 inches; length, 75 feet 2 inches; loaded weight, 78,000 pounds; engines, two 10,200-pounds-thrust Allison turbojets; maximum speed, more than 700 miles per hour.

Top: The B-66B could carry a hydrogen bomb. Center: The RB-66C was for electronic reconnaissance. Below: WB-66D's gathered accurate information about weather.

OTHER HISTORIC AIR FORCE BOMBERS

Above: The G.A.X. (Ground Attack Experimental) was designed by the Air Service. Boeing built ten, called GA-1. Below: The Air Corps ordered 13 Curtiss Y1A-18's.

Above: The gull-wing, all-metal Douglas XB-7 was advanced for 1931. Only seven were built. Below: Vultee's YA-19 of 1938. Seven of the planes were ordered.